4-08

D1103939

Mysterious Encounters

by Adam Woog

KIDHAVEN PRESS

An imprint of Thomson Gale, a part of The Thomson Corporation

THOMSON

━━★━━ ™

GALE

Detroit • New York • San Francisco • San Diego • New Haven, Conn. • Waterville, Maine • London • Munich

Thanks to David George Gordon and
Marg. Parsons for research help.

© 2006 Thomson Gale, a part of The Thomson Corporation.

Thomson and Star Logo are trademarks and Gale and KidHaven Press are registered
trademarks used herein under license.

For more information, contact
KidHaven Press
27500 Drake Rd.
Farmington Hills, MI 48331-3535
Or you can visit our Internet site at http://www.gale.com

Picture credits:

Cover photo: Joseph Paris/Brian V. Staples/Mark Sampson; Maury Aaseng, 7, 8; AP/Wide
World Photos, 17 (large photo), 18, 34; © Bettmann/CORBIS, 35; Cliff Crook/Fortean Picture
Library, 21; EPA/Landov, 31; Dr. Wolf Fahrenbach/Visuals Unlimited/Getty Images, 17 (inset);
Fortean Picture Library, 5, 12, 29; Ernst Haas/Hulton Archive/Getty Images, 40; Tony
Healy/Fortean Picture Library, 11; Mary Evans Picture Library, 15, 19, 26; Christopher L.
Murphy/Fortean Picture Library, 24; PhotoDisc, 30; Photo: Patterson/Gimlin, © 1968
Dahinden/René Dahinden/Fortean Picture Library, 37 (both photos); William M.
Rebsamen/Fortean Picture Library, 39; © Lawrence Schwartzwald. SYGMA/CORBIS, 9.

LIBRARY OF CONGRESS CATALOGING-IN-PUBLICATION DATA

Woog, Adam, 1953-
  Bigfoot / by Adam Woog.
    p. cm. — (Mysterious encounters)
  Includes bibliographical references and index.
  Contents: What is Bigfoot?—Encounters with the bashful Bigfoot—
Bigfoot attacks!—Hunting Bigfoot.
  ISBN 0-7377-3473-6 (hard cover : alk. paper) 1. Sasquatch—Juvenile literature.
I. Title. II. Series.
  QL89.2.S2W67 2006
  001.944—dc22

                                                             2005025524

Printed in the United States of America

Contents

Chapter 1

S trange and unknown creatures that look like giant apes may be living deep in the woods of North America. People have been claiming to see these mysterious beasts, called Bigfoot, for hundreds of years, and new sightings are reported all the time. One group that studies the creatures says it gets about half a dozen new Bigfoot reports every day!

Some people say that Bigfoot does not exist. In their opinion, people claiming to see Bigfoot creatures are really seeing animals such as bears, or else they are being fooled by human tricksters. However, many people, including serious researchers, are convinced that the stories about Bigfoot are true.

Are huge, unidentified beasts really roaming the wilderness regions of Canada and the United States? No one knows for sure. There have been thousands of reported sightings of creatures, and evidence such as huge, unexplained footprints has been found. Yet so far no one has found complete and certain proof.

This painting shows one artist's view of what Bigfoot might look like.

No Flesh or Bones

Nobody has ever found a Bigfoot carcass, which would be proof positive that the creatures really exist. As a reporter for the Akron, Ohio, *Beacon Journal* comments, "We have no Sasquatch flesh; we have no Sasquatch bones."

So the question remains open. David George Gordon, a nature writer and the author of the *Field Guide to the Sasquatch*, says that he is still undecided. Gordon comments, "If I said that Bigfoot doesn't exist, and someone discovers one tomorrow. . . . Well. However, I certainly wouldn't want to go to court with the evidence collected so far."[1]

What Is Bigfoot?

There are many theories about exactly what Bigfoot might be. Some people think that it is a type of early human. According to this theory, small groups of Bigfoot creatures may have somehow survived, without changing, from humankind's earliest stages of **evolution**.

However, most serious researchers think that Bigfoot might be a **primate**—that is, an ape. They suspect that the creature is related to a type of **extinct** ape that lived in Asia millions of years ago. If this is true, Bigfoot creatures are the only **species** of apes that still exists in North America.

No one knows how many Bigfoot creatures might exist today. One estimate puts the number at about 2,000. Most of them are thought to live in one region, the Pacific Northwest of the United States and western Canada. This area includes northern California, Washington, Oregon, and the Canadian provinces of British Columbia and the Yukon Territory.

Believers think that most Bigfoot creatures are in this region because most of the reported sightings come from there. However, people have filed reports about Bigfoot creatures from every province in Canada and from nearly every state in America.

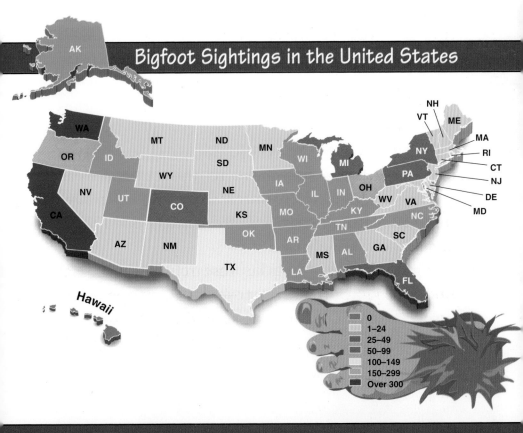

Bigfoot Sightings in the United States

- 0
- 1–24
- 25–49
- 50–99
- 100–149
- 150–299
- Over 300

Sasquatch (Canada and United States)

GREENLAND

Yeti (Asia)

NORTH AMERICA

ASIA

Am Fear Liath Mor (Scotland)

EUROPE

Bigfoot (United States)

MIDDLE EAST

Hibagon (Japan)

Skunk Ape (Florida)

AFRICA

Swamp Goblin (Louisiana)

SOUTH AMERICA

Nguoi Rung (Vietnam)

Abominable Snowman (Himalayas)

Red-Haired Mountain Man (Eastern United States)

Mapinguari (Brazil)

Kikomba (Africa)

AUSTRALIA

Yowie (Australia)

Depending on the region, the creature can have different names. For example, in the Pacific Northwest, Bigfoot is also called Sasquatch. This name comes from a Native American word that means "wild man" or "hairy man." In other regions, Bigfoot goes by other colorful names, including Swamp Goblin, Red-haired Mountain Man, and Skunk Ape.

Big and Tall

Reports of Bigfoot creatures suggest that they are very different from each other in the ways they look and act. In fact, the creatures seem to be nearly as individual in their looks and actions as humans. However, just as all humans are somewhat alike, all Bigfoot creatures seem to share some common characteristics.

For example, Bigfoot creatures are all reported to have two arms and two legs, just like apes and humans. Also, they are said to be big—very big! Reports indicate that the adult Bigfoot, on average, is about 7 feet, 10 inches (2.38m), although many individuals are even taller. The tallest professional basketball player of all time, Gheorghe Muresan of the Washington Bullets, was only 7 feet, 7 inches (2.3m) tall!

Bigfoot creatures are also reported to be physically powerful. Believers say they are strong and can

An average Bigfoot creature is said to be taller than former professional basketball player Gheorghe Muresan, pictured here on a movie set.

run fast and jump over fences easily. Furthermore, they are thought to weigh a lot. The average adult's weight has been estimated at about 650 pounds (294.85kg). That is about as heavy as two professional football players put together!

"Bigfoot" Is an Accurate Name

Bigfoot sightings suggest that the creatures have other characteristics in common as well. For example, they are always said to be covered in hair (not fur). This hair is especially thick on their heads and across their shoulders. It can be white or black, but usually it is brown. This brown can be light, medium, or dark.

Also, Bigfoot creatures are reported to walk upright on two legs. They take long steps and run fast, usually hunched over. They have large, barrel-shaped chests and make heavy breathing noises when they run. Bigfoot creatures also have very long arms. Their hands are broad, with long fingers and short thumbs.

A typical Bigfoot's head is described as small compared to the bulky size of its body. Its face has strong, heavy eyebrow ridges and deep-set brown eyes. Bigfoot creatures also have square, strong teeth, heavy jaws, flattened noses, and ears hidden under thick hair. And a Bigfoot also smells really bad. The odor is reported to be strong enough to make people want to throw up.

Of course, Bigfoot creatures also have big feet— very big! Studies of supposed Bigfoot tracks show that the creature's feet usually have four or five toes each and are at least 14 inches (35.56cm) long and 6 inches (15.24cm) wide—much bigger than the feet of even the biggest human or ape. An interesting thing about Bigfoot feet is that, unlike humans,

Flat Feet

Footprints are the most common type of Bigfoot evidence. A typical footprint is 16 to 18 inches (40.64 to 45.72cm) long, 7 inches (17.78cm) wide, and flat. No other creature is known to have a footprint like this.

A teen laughs at the size of plaster casts of footprints supposedly made by a Bigfoot creature.

The mysterious Bigfoot-like creature in this photo was spotted in Florida in 2000.

Bigfoot creatures apparently have no insteps—that is, their feet are completely flat.

Unanswered Questions

All of this information about how Bigfoot creatures look and act comes from thousands of reported encounters with Bigfoot. Sometimes the people who make these reports say they have actually seen the creatures. Sometimes, however, they simply have seen evidence that the creatures may exist.

This evidence can come in many forms. For example, people have seen footprints in mud and snow, or they have heard strange noises. Sometimes, they find bits of hair that do not seem to come from animals such as bears or wolves.

Reports about such findings have led researchers to make some conclusions about Bigfoot. However, there are still many unanswered questions about the mysterious creature and its habits. For instance, no one knows exactly what Bigfoot might eat. Some believers think that the beast is a **vegetarian**, eating only plants and roots. However, others think that Bigfoot is **omnivorous**. This means that the beasts may eat everything and anything, including fish and meat.

Obstacles

Such questions will never be answered unless researchers can collect more information. However, there are many obstacles to learning more. One major problem is that Bigfoot creatures seem to be generally shy.

They have not been reported as being especially frightened of people, and they are usually not violent. If they do happen to run into humans, they usually are said to ignore them or simply go away. However, Bigfoot creatures normally avoid human contact, staying far away from cities or towns. Because of this, most Bigfoot encounters have been brief glimpses of the mysterious creatures from a distance.

Chapter 2

Encounters with the Bashful Bigfoot

Stories about brief encounters with shy Bigfoot creatures—or reports of evidence—go back for hundreds of years. For example, the first known written report about a Bigfoot was in a British newspaper in 1784. It said that an unknown type of hairy, manlike beast had been briefly spotted in the woods of the Canadian province of Manitoba.

Many other similar stories followed. For example, in 1811 a fur trader named David Thompson said that he found strange footprints in deep snow near what is now Jasper, Alberta, in the Canadian Rocky Mountains. He said that each foot had four toes and was about 14 inches (35.56cm) long and

8 inches (20.32cm) wide. Thompson noted that these prints were much too large to have been human or bear tracks.

A Yukon Sighting

Reports of glimpsing the bashful Bigfoot have been made ever since. One recent sighting occurred in June 2004 in the Yukon Territory of northwest Canada. Marion Sheldon and Gus Jules, who live in

High in the Himalaya Mountains, two explorers and their guides examine mysterious footprints.

the tiny village of Teslin, were driving down the Alaska-Yukon Highway at night. They spotted what they thought was a person near the construction site of the village's new airport.

The men turned around, thinking that they had seen someone from the village who might need help. However, when they got close they realized that what they saw was not a person at all! It was a human-shaped thing, about 7 feet (2.3m) tall and completely covered in hair. This strange creature clearly did not want to be near humans. It moved away quickly, and it needed just two steps to completely cross the wide highway. Then it vanished into the woods.

Sheldon and Jules reported their sighting to the local authorities the next day. But any possible footprints had already been destroyed by rain. Also, word had spread quickly about the strange incident. By the time the authorities got there, many people were on the scene and had trampled all over the area. The only evidence the authorities could save was a small sample of what might have been Bigfoot hair.

Scientific Testing

The authorities were undecided about exactly what had occurred. Dave Bakica, a conservation officer for the region, comments, "[The two men] are pretty shook up over it. I have no doubt in my mind that they believe what they saw was a sas-

A scientist holds a sample of what may be Bigfoot hair. In the picture at left, a possible Bigfoot hair is magnified many times.

quatch. Whether it was or not, I do not know. Just because you can't prove something was there, does not mean it was not there."[2]

Bigfoot fans everywhere were excited about the sighting. However, scientific testing of the evidence left behind was disappointing. DNA analysis of the hair proved that it was actually fur from a bison, an animal similar to a buffalo that is native to the region.

Bigfoot Country

Willow Creek, California, calls itself "the Capital of Bigfoot Country." The town's museum has a 25-foot (7.62m) wooden Bigfoot statue, casts of footprints, a handprint, and other evidence of the massive ape-man.

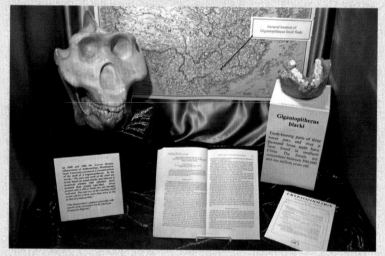

A display at California's Willow Creek Museum features a replica of what may be a Bigfoot skull.

Many residents of Teslin still believe that a Bigfoot was sighted. According to a reporter for the Canadian Broadcasting Company, "It will take more than a DNA test on a bit of bison fur to shake some Teslin residents' belief that they have a sasquatch in the neighbourhood."[3]

Curious Creatures

Sometimes, Bigfoot creatures seem to be curious as well as shy. For example, a sighting was reported in May 2005 in northern California's remote Del Norte County. Late one afternoon, two teenage girls from a local tribe of Native Americans, the Yuroks, took a break while driving on a remote road.

They were sitting on the hood of their truck, talking and laughing, when they both began to feel

In this fanciful painting, a Bigfoot watches scientists who are following its tracks.

strange. Suddenly, a very large manlike thing walked out of the woods and onto the side of road. It stood very still, looking at the girls. They said it had gray-black hair all over its body, the shoulders of a giant, huge hands and fingers, dark skin, and an ugly face.

Terrified, the girls stared at the creature. It stared back and twisted its hands together as if it were nervous. The girls decided to get back in the truck. They moved very slowly off the hood, got in, and locked the doors. When they looked again, the creature was gone.

The girls went home and told their grand-mother about the incident. She said they had seen what she called a creek devil. The grandmother said the creature did not mean them harm. It was sim-ply curious about their giggling.

A Believer

Still another incident about a shy Bigfoot was re-ported by nature writer Robert Michael Pyle in his 1995 book *Where Bigfoot Walks*. It concerned a man named Jim Fielder. Fielder had been a biology

Bigfoot or Chimpanzee?

In 1884 a Canadian newspaper reported the capture of "Jacko," a strong manlike creature covered with black hair. It may have been a chimpanzee brought from Africa by a sailor, but some people believed it was a Sasquatch.

Some people believe this picture, taken in Washington State in 1995, is proof that Bigfoot is real. Other people, however, believe the picture is a fake.

teacher for many years and did not believe in Bigfoot. However, his opinion changed one night when he was driving near Mount Rainier in Washington State's rugged Cascade Mountains.

Fielder rounded a curve and saw something lying in the middle of the highway, about 100 yards (91.44m) ahead of his car. He thought at first it was a deer, an elk, or another large wild animal. He thought that maybe it was lying in the road because it was wounded.

But when Fielder was about 50 yards (45.72m) away, the creature got up. As he got close, Fielder thought for sure it was a bear—it was reddish brown, the right color for the type of bears often seen near Mount Rainier at that time of year. But then it stood up on two legs and lumbered off toward the forest, taking at least ten steps upright—something no bear can do.

The creature disappeared into the woods as Fielder drove past. He estimated that it was between 6 and 6.5 feet (1.83 and 1.98m) tall, was very bulky, and had long arms. He could not see its face.

Fielder hoped to return later and look for evidence, but he was called away on a family medical emergency and could not get back. Nonetheless, Fielder says that night he became a believer in the legendary creature. He remarked, "I'm . . . the last biologist who would believe in Bigfoot. But that night I went from a Bigfoot agnostic [nonbeliever] to a Bigfoot born-again [believer] in ten seconds."[4]

Sometimes Aggressive

These stories represent just a few of the reported sightings of Bigfoot over the years. In the vast majority of reports, the creatures are shy and not aggressive. However, there are exceptions to this general rule. Occasionally, if a Bigfoot has been injured or threatened, an encounter can turn violent. It can even be dangerous!

Chapter 3

Bigfoot Attacks!

There are not many reports about aggressive or violent Bigfoot creatures. However, they do sometimes occur. Back in the 1850s, for instance, some gold prospectors in California claimed that Bigfoot creatures attacked them and destroyed their equipment.

There have been many similar reports over the years. For example, in 1902 in Chesterfield, Idaho, some people out skating were attacked by a hairy monster with a wooden club. They said the creature was about 8 feet (2.44m) tall. In 1977 in Wantage, New Jersey, the Sites family reported seeing a huge Bigfoot with brown hair and red, glowing eyes. It broke into their barn, killed several of their rabbits, and swatted

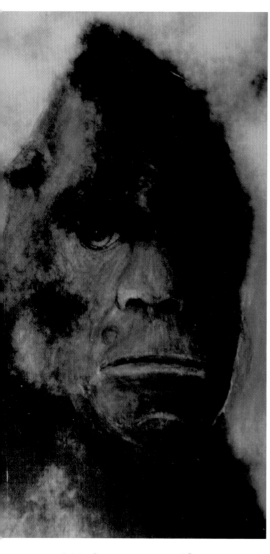

This illustration shows an artist's idea of what Bigfoot might look like up close.

their dog, sending it flying about 20 feet (6.1m).

Other incidents have been reported from all over the country. On several occasions in the 1970s, for example, a Bigfoot creature was reported chasing cattle near Skipperville, Alabama. And in 1983 a family in Oklahoma reported that a Bigfoot attacked their house, knocking out windows, beating on the walls, and trying to tear the back door off.

Kidnapped!

One well-known story dates from 1924. A logger, Albert Ostman, claimed that a Sasquatch family kidnapped him. Ostman was camping and prospecting for gold near Toba Inlet, British Columbia, when something began disturbing his camp and stealing food during the night.

Ostman thought a porcupine was the culprit, and he set a trap to catch it. He was quite surprised, then, when it turned out to be a male Bigfoot! Ostman said the giant creature picked him up while he was sleeping, holding him in his sleeping bag like a sack of potatoes. The creature also took Ostman's supplies.

The creature carried and dragged his load over the mountains to a deep valley, where he rejoined his Bigfoot family. In addition to the Bigfoot father, who had kidnapped Ostman, a mother, a son, and a daughter were in this family. They were all very curious about Ostman and made him stay in the valley. Every day, the mother and children looked for food, mostly roots and grass, while the father guarded the logger. If Ostman tried to walk away, the father moved his arms threateningly and pushed him down.

Bigfoot's Name

The name "Bigfoot" was coined in 1958, when a California bulldozer operator named Jerry Crew said he found enormous footprints near a job site. This story became famous, but it was recently revealed that Crew's sighting was a hoax.

Although Bigfoot creatures are usually said to be shy, some have reportedly attacked humans.

Ostman says he escaped after six days because the father became very interested in the logger's snuff, which is a kind of tobacco. The father Sasquatch ate an entire box of snuff from Ostman's knapsack. It made the creature very thirsty, and when he went looking for water Ostman was able to escape.

The man walked downhill until he came to a logging camp. The people there helped him get back home. However, Ostman kept his story a secret for many years. He did not tell anyone about the Bigfoot family until 1957, because he feared that no one would believe him.

Revenge of the Bigfoot

Another famous incident also occurred in 1924. Five prospectors near Mount St. Helens in southwest Washington State reported that they saw strange tracks and caught glimpses of several unidentifiable creatures. According to a Portland, Oregon, newspaper the *Oregonian*, "The animals were said to have the appearance of huge gorillas. They are covered with long, black hair. Their ears are about 4 inches [10.16cm] long and stick straight up. Their tracks are 13 to 14 inches [33 to 35.6cm] long."[5]

One of the prospectors shot at the creatures with his rifle and may have wounded one of them. That night, a group of Bigfoot creatures attacked the prospectors' log cabin, bombarding it with rocks.

The rocks knocked chunks out of the cabin and hit one man so hard that he was knocked unconscious.

According to the prospectors, the creatures came very close, pounding on the cabin walls and trying to get in. At one point, a Bigfoot reached through an opening in the wall and nearly snatched an ax away from one of the men. The prospector escaped serious injury by firing his gun through the hole in the wall, which forced the creature to give up the ax.

The prospectors said they fought the animals all night. They then packed up their things and left the cabin. However, when people went to the cabin later to check on the story, there was no sign of a struggle or of any creatures. In the *Field Guide to the Sasquatch*, Gordon notes, "A search party dispatched to the scene of the incident found no signs of Sasquatches or any other giant, apelike beings."[6] Nonetheless, the story about giant creatures has persisted, and the site of the cabin is still called Ape Canyon.

The Incident at Ruby Creek

Another strange incident occurred in 1941. It happened to the Chapmans, a family of Native Canadians who lived in a place called Ruby Creek in British Columbia. The family consisted of George and Jeannie Chapman and their four children.

At about three o'clock on a sunny day, the oldest Chapman boy, who was nine, came running to the house to tell his mother that a strange creature was coming out of the nearby woods. The other children were playing outdoors, and George Chapman was away at work on the railroad.

Jeannie Chapman went out to look. At first she thought a bear was moving in the bushes on the far side of a field behind their house. She immediately told the other children to come inside. Then she saw that it was no bear—it was a gigantic manlike

Hoaxes

Many supposed Bigfoot sightings have proven to be hoaxes. For instance, people have made "footprints" using fake wooden feet or altered boots. At least two movies of supposed sightings have also proven to be hoaxes.

This plaster cast was made of a footprint supposedly left by a Bigfoot creature in 1967.

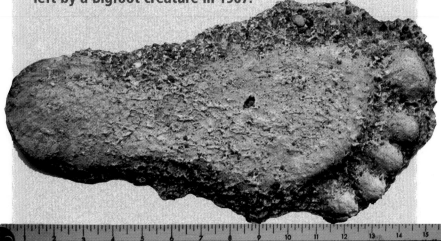

creature, about 7 feet (2m) tall and covered with pale yellow-brown hair.

The creature was coming quickly toward the house. Chapman stayed outside and told her oldest son to get a blanket. By the time he got it, the creature was only about 100 feet (30.48m) away. Chapman held the blanket up so that her children were hidden from the creature's sight.

Escaping from the Sasquatch

Chapman then led her children down to the river, and they followed it to the nearby village. When George Chapman came home from work, he saw that the door of his woodshed had been battered in. Enormous footprints were everywhere. Also, a huge 55-gallon (208.2l) metal barrel of salted fish had been broken open and its contents were scattered. Several long brown hairs were stuck in the doorway, far above the level of George Chapman's head.

Some researchers believe that people who have reported Bigfoot sightings were actually seeing bears.

Frightened, Chapman dashed around looking for his family. He spotted the tracks they had made going off toward the river and the village. He ran to the village and found them. Chapman then asked his father-in-law and two others to stay at the house for a while. They protected the Chapman family while he was at work.

Enormous footprints appeared near the Chapmans' house every night for a week, and on two occasions late at night the family's dogs howled and the family heard a strange, gurgling whistle. No one in the family ever saw a Bigfoot again, but the incident was so un-

Russian researchers search for evidence of Bigfoot in an area where a hairy leg unlike the leg of any known animal was found in 2003.

nerving that a week later the Chapmans moved away for good.

Similar stories about strange encounters with Bigfoot creatures have been reported more recently as well. Also in recent years, groups of people have banded together to scientifically search for the eerie animals. Some of these Bigfoot hunters say they have had close encounters with the creatures.

Chapter 4

Hunting Bigfoot

Most of the time, people meet Bigfoot by accident. Sometimes, however, people make trips into the wilderness especially to look for the creatures. Many of these people belong to organized groups that are devoted to researching Bigfoot. The largest of these is the Bigfoot Field Researchers Organization.

Most of the time on these trips, Bigfoot hunters look for evidence that they can study later. For example, they search for footprints or bits of hair. However, a number of hunters report a much more thrilling experience—a close, personal encounter with one of the creatures.

These dramatic meetings convince Bigfoot hunters of the truth of the creatures' existence. Don Keating, who heads the Eastern Ohio Bigfoot Investigation Center in Newcomerstown, Ohio, told a reporter for the Cleveland *Plain Dealer* newspaper, "I've seen the creature itself—September 15, 1985, 4 miles [6.44km] south of Newcomerstown, no more than 35 feet [10.67m] away. Within 10 miles [16km] of my own home, I've seen footprints. It's really difficult to doubt your own eyes."[7]

Different Kinds of Evidence

Some of these hunters are able to take videos or photos of what appear to be Bigfoot creatures. Also, they sometimes make recordings of **vocalizations** (the whooping, screaming sounds that Bigfoot creatures are reported to make).

At other times, Bigfoot hunters find evidence that indicates only that the creatures were there in

A Heavy Load

When Bigfoot hunters take trips to look for the creature, they carry lots of equipment. Among their tools are notebooks, video and still cameras, tape recorders, and equipment for making casts of footprints.

This picture is from a movie shot in 1977 and supposedly shows a Bigfoot creature in northern California.

the past. The most common piece of evidence of this type is a footprint. Hunters take plaster casts of these apparent footprints, preserving them for study later. Other examples of this sort of evidence include scat (feces) and the remains of shelters that Bigfoot creatures are believed to have built from tree branches and other materials.

The Sasquatch on Film

One close, personal encounter by a hunter resulted in the world's most famous piece of evidence about Bigfoot. This is a short movie that captures what

A hunter poses with a seventeen-inch-long footprint he found near Coos Bay, Oregon.

seems to be a 7-foot (2.13m), apelike creature in the mountains of northern California.

The man who took this movie was named Roger Patterson. He was an experienced Bigfoot researcher who wanted to make a documentary film about the creature. On October 20, 1967, he and his friend Bob Gimlin were riding horses in California's remote Bluff Creek region.

Suddenly, they spotted a huge dark-haired creature hunched over in the middle of a creek. As they watched, the beast rose to its full height, which the men estimated at 7 feet, 4 inches (2.2m). It was apparently a female. She began walking away from the men and toward the woods.

Important Evidence

Even though his frightened horse reared and threw him to the ground, Patterson was able to pull a movie camera from his saddlebag. Patterson filmed as best he could. There was only enough film left in the camera to record the alleged Bigfoot very briefly. Patterson's movie is less than a minute long.

The film caused a great sensation among Bigfoot hunters, and in the years since it has been carefully examined and analyzed. According to one such analysis by researcher Christopher L. Murphy, the movie shows that the creature acted normally until it realized that the two men were looking at it. Murphy writes, "It does not appear that the creature . . . felt immediately threatened until it

These pictures of an apelike creature in northern California are from the famous film shot by Roger Patterson in 1967.

turns and looks at Patterson—about one-third of the time into the filming. At this point the creature [speeds up] as it continued its passage."[8]

Some people think that the creature on the film was not a real Bigfoot. They claim that the movie was faked—that the Bigfoot was really a man in a specially made ape suit. However, Patterson's film is accepted as authentic by many Bigfoot researchers.

Bigfoot Law

Even though Bigfoot's existence is unproven, some local governments protect the creatures by law. For instance, it is forbidden to hunt Bigfoot on land belonging to the Sioux. Also, it is illegal to kill a Bigfoot in Skamania County, Washington. The penalty is a $1,000 fine and five years in jail!

Screams in the Valley

Another example of a researcher having a firsthand encounter with a Bigfoot came in 2005. Paul Graves, a longtime researcher based in Wenatchee, Washington, was camping with another Bigfoot hunter near Stevens Pass in the Cascade Mountains of Washington State. They were on a Sasquatch-hunting expedition.

Suddenly, in the middle of the night, they were awakened from their sleep by a long, piercing cry. It was like a woman's scream, Graves said, but it also had whooping breaths like some apes make. He told a reporter for the *Wenatchee World* newspaper, "We just looked at each other in disbelief. We heard it scream twice. It wasn't close, but it had the volume [loudness] to carry across the valley."[9]

Still another incident was witnessed by one of the best known of Bigfoot hunters, Jeff Meldrum, an anatomy professor at Idaho State University. Meldrum was on a trip to collect casts of Bigfoot prints when his campsite was disturbed and footprints were left.

The culprit, according to Meldrum, was not a bear or any other well-known creature. Meldrum told a Spokane, Washington, reporter, "We found our food stolen and packs rifled without the typical signs associated with bears. A **biped** [two-legged animal] unmistakably left the footprints."[10]

People who claim to have seen Bigfoot creatures say they walk upright on two legs as humans do.

A "Blurry Blackness"

In 2005 a group of experienced Bigfoot hunters reported seeing a dozen huge tracks next to a logging road near Clover Mountain in northern California's rugged Shasta County. They went back three days later to make plaster casts of the prints, and at that time one hunter, Tom Biscardi, claimed to see the beast itself. Biscardi said he heard rustling in the brush but thought at first that it was snow melting from treetops.

He was surprised to look up and see a "blurry blackness" that "wasn't deer. It wasn't a bear. It was unbelievable." It stood upright about 100 yards (91.44m) away from him. He told a reporter, "I said, 'Oh God, here it is again.'" (This was Biscardi's fifth sighting in 32 years of Bigfoot hunting.) "I'm yelling to the guys, 'Come on, get the cameras, let's go!'"[11]

No one was able to film the event, however. Also, Biscardi did not have a **tranquilizer** gun or other equipment he could have used to capture the creature. He said that all he could do was throw a stick at the creature, hoping to make it angry. However, the Bigfoot did not get angry. It simply disappeared into the trees.

Although some people believe this preserved skull and hand belonged to a Bigfoot creature, there is still no conclusive evidence that such creatures exist.

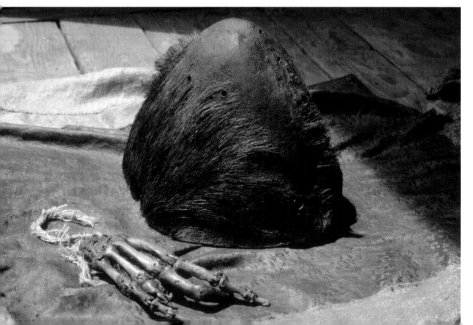

The Search Continues

These are just a few of the many stories reported by dedicated researchers who have spent countless hours hunting for Bigfoot. Along the way, they have collected a huge amount of evidence. Nonetheless, there is still no definite proof that Bigfoot exists.

People will continue to question the existence of Bigfoot until one of the creatures can be captured or killed. However, no one has ever found the dead body of a Bigfoot, much less brought one back for study. This may not ever happen. Many Bigfoot experts feel that killing one of the creatures would be a crime as bad as murder.

The controversy will no doubt continue into the future. Dedicated Bigfoot researchers, as well as ordinary people who just happen to be out in the woods, will continue to report sightings and find evidence. And so the elusive, mysterious, and exciting creatures will continue to hover in the public imagination—just out of sight!

Notes

Chapter One: What Is Bigfoot?

1. David George Gordon, e-mail to author, August 21, 2005.

Chapter Two: Encounters with the Bashful Bigfoot

2. Quoted in Chuck Tobin, "Witnesses 'Shook Up' over Creature Sighting," *Whitehorse Daily Star*, June 11, 2004. www.whitehorse star.com/auth.php?r=33451.
3. Quoted in *CBC North*, "Teslinites Remain Faithful to Idea of Local Bigfoot," July 29, 2005. http://north.cbc.ca/regional/servlet/View?filename=teslin-sasquatch-29072005.
4. Quoted in Robert Michael Pyle, *Where Bigfoot Walks: Crossing the Dark Divide*. Boston: Houghton Mifflin, 1995, p. 107.

Chapter Three: Bigfoot Attacks!

5. Quoted in David George Gordon, *Field Guide to the Sasquatch*. Seattle: Sasquatch, 1992, p. 20.
6. Gordon, *Field Guide to the Sasquatch*, p. 21.

7. Quoted in Tom Feran, "Bigfoot Hunters Still on Their Toes," *Cleveland Plain Dealer,* February 2, 2003. www.rfthomas.clara.net/news/ontoes.html.
8. Christopher L. Murphy, *Meet the Sasquatch.* Blaine, WA: Hancock House, 2004, p. 42.
9. Quoted in Rick Steigmeyer, "Keeping an Eye Out for Bigfoot," *Wenatchee World,* February 26, 2005. www.spokesmanreview.com/local/story.asp?ID=56271.
10. Quoted in Dan Gallagher, "Professor Wants Answer to Bigfoot Question—Endless Topic for Research and Hook for His Students," *Spokane* (WA) *Spokesman-Review,* May 15, 1999. www.oregonbigfoot.com/articles/meldrum_01.php.
11. Quoted in Alex Breitler, "Bigfoot Sighting Leaves Lasting Imprint," *Redding* (CA) *Record Searchlight,* April 16, 2005. www.bigfootencounters.com/articles/burney05.htm.

Glossary

biped: An animal that walks on two feet.

evolution: The theory that animals have evolved, or changed, over millions of years.

extinct: Not existing any longer.

omnivorous: An animal or person able to eat meat and fish as well as plants and vegetables.

primate: The classification of mammal that includes humans and apes.

species: A group of animals that can breed with each other (such as dogs, cats, or monkeys).

tranquilizer: A drug that makes people or animals sleepy or calm.

vegetarian: A person who eats only vegetables.

vocalizations: Sounds made with the voice.

For Further Exploration

Books

Julie S. Bach, *Exploring the Unknown: Bigfoot.* San Diego: Lucent, 1995. This is written for slightly older readers, but it has good photos.

Michael Burgan, *The Unexplained: Bigfoot.* Mankato, MN: Capstone, 2005. This book is a good, brief introduction to the subject.

Brian Innes, *Giant Humanlike Beasts.* Austin, TX: Raintree Steck-Vaughn, 1999. Part of a series called Unsolved Mysteries, this book discusses Bigfoot and its cousins around the world, such as the yeti.

Elaine Landau, *Sasquatch: Wild Man of the Woods.* Brookfield, CT: Millbrook, 1993. A good introduction to the topic.

Video

Rasha Drachovitch, producer, *Bigfoot.* New York: New Video Group, 1994. An episode of A&E Channel's *Ancient Mysteries* series, this program includes interviews with Bigfoot experts, skeptics, and witnesses; it also reproduces much of the famous Patterson-Gimlin film.

Bigfoot Encounters (www.n2.net/prey/bigfoot). A site that records many alleged Bigfoot encounters. Under "Videos, Images, and Sounds," visitors to this site can look at and listen to clips of alleged Bigfoot sightings.

Bigfoot Field Researchers Organization (www.bfro.net). The Web site of the largest Bigfoot research group. Not designed specifically for kids, but with lots of excellent photos and other material.

Bigfoot Museum (www.bigfootmuseum.com). An entertaining and well-organized site with lots of information and photos.

The Cryptozoologist (www.lorencoleman.com/cabinet_home.html). A site maintained by Loren Coleman, one of the world's most prominent Bigfoot hunters. The information is written for adults, but there are lots of pictures of Bigfoot casts and more.

Index